WORDS OF INSPIRATION & REFLECTIONS

THE PREACHER & THE *Street Prophet*

UNTRUAN GRANT & REV. LARRY WALKER

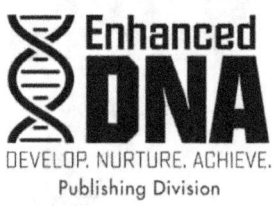

DEVELOP. NURTURE. ACHIEVE.
Publishing Division

The Preacher and the Street Prophet:
Words of Inspiration and Reflections

Copyright © 2021 Untruan Grant and
Rev. Larry G. Walker, Jr.
All rights reserved.

ISBN-13: 978-1-7360431-4-1
Library of Congress: 2021901744

The Preacher & The Street Prophet

DEDICATION – THE STREET PROPHET

UNTRUAN GRANT

Untruan Grant was born in the housing projects of Bon Ton, South Dallas. Born to Clifton Bishop & Tina Grant, he has always looked at life from his own lens; trusting his walk would be his greatest teacher. He is Founder & CEO of PMG Music Group, Lighthouse Media LLC, & Train 2 Heal Charms. Growing up in harsh and tough conditions, Untruan's mission is to live through the "impossible", to make his reality possible. He dedicates this book to his last living grandmother Betty Sims; the eyes of the family tree.

I found myself on a journey and a road that I knew my peers nor old friends could help. So, I turned to a program that I had enrolled in upon re-entering society that had been a great help. Mentoring had become a passion for me and it required going back through the program. It was there that I met Pastor Larry. After graduating the program, I felt his spirit and desire to help me; as he has done for so many others. I knew I needed a mentor and I embraced his support and love. From that point, I have grown to where I am today.

"All Things Are Possible".

DEDICATION – THE PREACHER

REV. LARRY WALKER, JR.

Rev. Larry G. Walker, Jr. is a tireless servant in the Dallas/Ft. Worth Metroplex for over 30+ years. He is the former Pastor of the Agape Baptist Community of Faith in Garland, Texas.

He and his wife, Robyn have been married for over 35 years and are the proud parents of two wonderful daughters, Charonne Kelyn Hadley and Dominique Symone Walker.

This book is dedicated to the memory of their daughter, Krysten Danielle Walker; who gained entrance into Heaven on January 14, 2020.

Her presence, smile and words were always inspirational and uplifting. No greater tribute can be given than, the contents of this book in her memory.

TABLE OF CONTENTS

DEDICATION – THE STREET PROPHET   *iv*

DEDICATION – THE PREACHER   *v*

ACKNOWLEDGMENTS   *xii*

1. *LEAVE A TRAIL*   *2*
2. *EARNING THEIR WAY*   *3*
3. *THANK YOU GOD*   *4*
4. *KNOW THAT YOU ARE*   *5*
5. *LOSING VS WINNING*   *6*
6. *LET THEM CRY*   *7*
7. *IT'S YOUR JOY*   *8*
8. *YOU ARE RESOURCEFUL*   *9*
9. *NOW IS MY TOMORROW*   *10*
10. *CLEANSING*   *11*
11. *GUARANTEES*   *12*
12. *THANKFUL IN LOSS*   *13*
13. *BROKENESS*   *14*
14. *THE DREAM*   *15*

15.	*IN TUNE*	**16**
16.	*PLANTING SEEDS*	**17**
17.	*BE PATIENT*	**18**
18.	*LAUGH*	**19**
19.	*REAL EYES*	**20**
20.	*DISCIPLINE*	**21**
21.	*A NEW DAY*	**22**
22.	*FRESH START*	**23**
23.	*FEAR*	**24**
24.	*DESTINY*	**25**
25.	*IDENTITY*	**26**
26.	*THE GPS SYSTEM*	**27**
27.	*KNOWING & WILLING*	**28**
28.	*INSIDE/OUT*	**29**
29.	*UNAPOLOGETIC*	**30**
30.	*CHOOSE WISELY*	**31**
31.	*THE LONG WAY*	**32**
32.	*LEAVE FOOTPRINTS*	**33**
33.	*WATCHING*	**34**
34.	*PAINT THE PICTURE*	**35**

35.	***BEST VERSION***	**36**
36.	***VISION & CLARITY***	**37**
37.	***WHAT MAKES YOU, U***	**38**
38.	***TIME IS NO FRIEND***	**39**
39.	***RESPECT TIME***	**40**
40.	***WILL POWER***	**41**
41.	***I AM GREAT***	**42**
42.	***DO IT!***	**43**
43.	***LAYERS***	**44**
44.	***CAPTURE MOMENTS***	**45**
45.	***MEMORY BANKS***	**46**
46.	***POTENTIAL***	**47**
47.	***DIMMER SWITCH***	**48**
48.	***SHINE ON***	**49**
49.	***YOUR LENS***	**50**
50.	***BREAKTHROUGH***	**51**
51.	***MAXIMUM POWER***	**52**
52.	***PREPARATION***	**53**
53.	***SHARE***	**54**
54.	***DREAMING***	**55**

55.	*WALK IT OUT*	**56**
56.	*OBSTACLES*	**57**
57.	*RENEWAL*	**58**
58.	*REWARDS*	**59**
59.	*WORK*	**60**
60.	*LAUGHTER*	**61**
61.	*TO BE GREAT*	**62**
62.	*BE A LIGHT*	**63**
63.	*ACCEPT STRUGGLE*	**64**
64.	*BLESSING BURDEN*	**65**
65.	*DREAM REALITY*	**66**
66.	*DO YOU WANT IT?*	**67**
67.	*THE BEST THINGS*	**68**
68.	*START ANEW*	**69**
69.	*A BLESSED NEW DAY*	**70**
70.	*YOUTHFULNESS*	**71**
71.	*RESPECT TIME*	**72**
72.	*RE-CREATE*	**73**
73.	*BE POSITIVE*	**74**
74.	*NEW THINGS*	**75**

75.	*SELFCARE*	**76**
76.	*STAND FIRM*	**77**
77.	*UNLOCKING DOORS*	**78**
78.	*LESSONS*	**79**
79.	*THE END*	**80**
	ABOUT THE AUTHOR	**82**
	ABOUT THE AUTHOR	**84**

ACKNOWLEDGMENTS

Rev. Larry Walker, Jr. and Untruan Grant wish to acknowledge the many lessons and inspiration from family and friends across the years and miles that have been crucial to the formulation of this book. Without your Love, Support and Encouragement, this project would have never been possible. We thank God for each and every one of you and the contributions you have made to our lives.

To generations that have gone before us, we salute you.
To the current generation, we embrace you.
To the future generation, we await you.

Special Photography credits to Mr. Maquis English of filmkings3.

A very special "Thank You" to Mrs. Denola Burton, Founder/CEO of Enhanced DNA Publishing for her expertise and friendship in making this pursuit happen.

TRAINsition 2 HEAL

Inspired Words by Untruan Grant

Reflections by Pastor Larry Walker

1. LEAVE A TRAIL

The Prophet:

"Walk through a field with no path and leave a trail...not to be found, but to show others that even they can create another way."

Untruan Grant

The Preacher:

Some people choose to follow a path that has already been created. Sure, it is easy ... but not nearly as adventurous. A path, a trail, a road – develop or choose whatever you want. I say create it that it might not just be found; but as proof that anyone can do it, if you just keep taking one step at a time.

Rev. Larry Walker, Jr.

2. EARNING THEIR WAY

The Prophet:

"Wanting associates is like desiring fans... keep them at a distance, you'll see who earns their way to be close."

Untruan Grant

The Preacher:

Desiring to have people like you, but who may not be like you, may create distance between you. Get to know people who are your true fans and they will inevitably be the closest ones to you.

Rev. Larry Walker, Jr.

3. THANK YOU GOD

The Prophet:

"Every time you say thank you to God...you welcome in the offering of your life, to exist in this realm of Heaven on Earth."

Untruan Grant

The Preacher

Thank you is the proper response when someone has done something good to or for you, given a blessing over your life or given a gift. Each breath you take should be followed "Thank You". Your life is a gift; what you do with it, is the return on investment that is received by the giver.

Rev. Larry Walker, Jr.

4. KNOW THAT YOU ARE

The Prophet:

"Never think that you're not...know that you are!!"

Untruan Grant

The Preacher:

Never accept the musings of those who remind you of what you are not. Be proud of what and who you are. You are the sum total of all your mistakes and all that seems to be your accomplishments.

Rev. Larry Walker, Jr.

5. LOSING VS WINNING

The Prophet:

"Losing does not mean you're not a winner. It just means you haven't found the right solution at this time."

Untruan Grant

The Preacher:

Losing does not determine who you are or define you. It just means the process has not been completed. Success is failures that became the foundation for what you are yet building.

Rev. Larry Walker, Jr.

6. LET THEM CRY

The Prophet:

"At some point you must get tired of crying other people's tears and allow them to cry their own."

Untruan Grant

The Preacher:

We all cry at times for other people. We take their punishment at times; even those they so rightly deserve. Crying is a cleansing emotional outlet. But only the tears of the proper one who owns their situation, can create the change needed to allow tears to be the watering tool necessary for growth.

Rev. Larry Walker, Jr.

7. IT'S YOUR JOY

The Prophet:

"You'll never have the joys of your life, always trying to live out the joys of other people's lives for them."

Untruan Grant

The Preacher:

You will miss the joy that is the essence of your life, trying to ensure joyful experiences in someone else's life. Rejoice with people, without sacrificing your own joy. Shared experiences are the best...but make sure someone is sharing yours with you.

Rev. Larry Walker, Jr.

8. YOU ARE RESOURCEFUL

The Prophet:

"Don't just look to others for an opportunity, and not to yourself. You're just as resourceful."

Untruan Grant

The Preacher:

Don't believe the lie that says you have nothing of value to contribute...no worthwhile ideas or ingenuity. Opportunities happen every day! It is up to you to recognize your own.

Rev. Larry Walker, Jr.

9. NOW IS MY TOMORROW

The Prophet:

*"The representation of my "now" is my tomorrow;
for that is the vision seen of myself today."*

Untruan Grant

The Preacher:

Looking to the future may allow me to miss the vision for me today. I live expectantly today because I know my yesterday brought me to this day.

Rev. Larry Walker, Jr.

10. CLEANSING

The Prophet:

"Staying Able means you must remove "cleanse" all the "toxins" out of your life continuously."

Untruan Grant

The Preacher:

Being available *and fit* to meet whatever you may face, requires continual cleansing of the mind, body and soul. I am able and available, when I have been thoroughly cleansed.

Rev. Larry Walker, Jr.

11. GUARANTEES

The Prophet:

"There is no good in making guarantees with others, when you've never first given yourself a guarantee."

Untruan Grant

The Preacher:

Only a few things in life can be guaranteed. We offer only a promise. Your guarantee must be a promise to yourself to do all that you can to always make something positive happen.

Rev. Larry Walker, Jr.

12. THANKFUL IN LOSS

The Prophet:

"Being thankful for what you feel you have lost, is showing gratitude for what you know is coming."

Untruan Grant

The Preacher:

To be thankful in loss, is to have confidence that something greater is coming. Trust in the one to whom you give thanks and remember to do so at all times.

Rev. Larry Walker, Jr.

13. BROKENESS

The Prophet:

"Your broken state is your open state to learn how to love; not broken but open."

Untruan Grant

The Preacher:

Brokenness allows us to be open to new adventures and opportunities IF we allow the brokenness to become one part of the process and not a final destination.

Rev. Larry Walker, Jr.

14. THE DREAM

The Prophet:

"Stay committed to the dream!...What you see up ahead, you will appreciate in the walk."

Untruan Grant

The Preacher:

Your good days will come & go...although your best days are always ahead and awaiting you. Sleep is just rest before making a dream reality.

Rev. Larry Walker, Jr.

15. IN TUNE

The Prophet:

"At times you are more in tune than you know, yet act out of tune listening to those surrounding you, rather than your inner self...the wavelength of the company kept."

Untruan Grant

The Preacher:

Be true to yourself and discerning of the situations and people around you...You have been given an incredible inner guide. Trust your instincts.

Rev. Larry Walker, Jr.

16. PLANTING SEEDS

The Prophet:

"If it's something you need to plant, get away from the concrete and find rich soil. You'll have a better chance to grow."

Untruan Grant

The Preacher:

Sometimes you have to breakthrough in order to grow. At other times...maybe you shouldn't make it so very difficult. Plant where there is less conflict. Easier is not always less valuable.

Rev. Larry Walker, Jr.

17. BE PATIENT

The Prophet:

"Be patient. At times you must go through what seems the worst in you, in order to get to the best of you."

Untruan Grant

The Preacher:

Take your time. Don't rush. You must experience what may seem like the worst, to achieve what is best. You learn from every mistake and grow with every attempt.

Rev. Larry Walker, Jr.

18. LAUGH

The Prophet:

"The more time you spend laughing the more time you spend healing. So, laugh often daily."

Untruan Grant

The Preacher:

Laugh hard and looong. Invest time in making your belly jiggle. It not only changes your facial expression, but also your attitude complexion.

Rev. Larry Walker, Jr.

19. REAL EYES

The Prophet:

"Real eyes do not give attention to what is in back or besides them because they're too busy looking at what's ahead of them...the future."

Untruan Grant

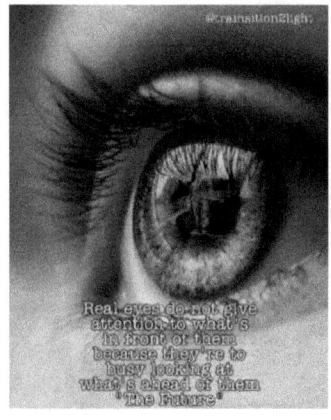

The Preacher:

To look deeply into what will be, you must train your eyes to ignore what is beside or behind you. Your future awaits. Keep your real eyes wide open!

Rev. Larry Walker, Jr.

20. DISCIPLINE

The Prophet:

"Focus is a discipline to help you hit your target, mark, or goal...it keeps you in sync with where you see your future self. So, stay focused on you."

Untruan Grant

The Preacher:

Hone in...sharpen your aim...Squint if you must. Every detail will make a difference. Your attention to the little things will propel you to hit the target; that is a better you.

Rev. Larry Walker, Jr.

21. A NEW DAY

The Prophet:

"Be as new as the new day & know life has something special awaiting you...reach out, rise up & be as bright as the sun so you don't miss it."

Untruan Grant

The Preacher:

A unique and heretofore never experienced awakening brings something very exciting and special. Reach out with both hands and grab an experience as big and glowing as the sun. Please don't miss it.

Rev. Larry Walker, Jr.

22. FRESH START

The Prophet:

"Get fresh & start fresh. It's a new day & so are you; unless you choose to hold onto the luggage of yesterday."

Untruan Grant

The Preacher:

Carrying unnecessary baggage can make you weary and tired, burdened and worn. Enjoy the journey of life and start each day renewed and refreshed. There is nothing like the feeling after a luxurious shower.

Rev. Larry Walker, Jr.

23. FEAR

The Prophet:

"Do not allow your fears to maximize your limitations; the sky is as endless as your limits should be...On the other side of fear is your destiny. Reach for it."

Untruan Grant

The Preacher:

It is normal to have fears. Do not let fear paralyze or make you stagnant. You will never conquer what you are unwilling to face. Un-limit your limits. There is something more even beyond the sky.

Rev. Larry Walker, Jr.

24. DESTINY

The Prophet:

"When it seem as you lost directions, begin to walk with your heart without fear...It will guide you along the journey of your life".

Untruan Grant

The Preacher:

Being lost, sometimes just means you do not recognize where you are. Our internal compass will always point us to our pre-ordained destination.

Rev. Larry Walker, Jr.

25. IDENTITY

The Prophet:

"Sometimes...maybe most times, you must lose yourself to find yourself...It's okay. You'll find you got it in you to map out this life".

Untruan Grant

The Preacher:

We get sidetracked and lose our way and even ourselves at times. Our identity and destiny is formed in the journey.

Rev. Larry Walker, Jr.

26. THE GPS SYSTEM

The Prophet:

"Allow your eyes to stay focused on what you see...not how you see it being done. You are the vehicle; God is the GPS."

Untruan Grant

The Preacher:

To remained focused, is one of the most difficult things in life; especially when we are our own navigator. Give control to the eternal GPS system. He never fails to get you home.

Rev. Larry Walker, Jr.

27. KNOWING & WILLING

The Prophet:

"Your job is to know <u>what</u> you see in yourself & allow the Devine to deal with the <u>how</u>… Just be willing to move on it and go."

Untruan Grant

The Preacher:

Ours is not to know the entire path and plan, but to move when told. A willing heart makes the journey possible and pleasant. A submitted heart makes it pleasurable.

Rev. Larry Walker, Jr.

28. INSIDE/OUT

The Prophet:

"The definition of who you are will always show on the outside...Be sure it's crystal clear; because it is how you will be viewed."

Untruan Grant

The Preacher:

The overflow of the internal is the outward expression seen on the outside. Make sure how people view you is the result of careful crafting of the picture you want to present.

Rev. Larry Walker, Jr.

29. UNAPOLOGETIC

The Prophet:

"Be perfectly clear about who you are, so there is no misunderstanding...You are who you are for a purpose. Live in it unapologetically."

Untruan Grant

The Preacher:

Uniqueness is an under-appreciated quality. Fitting in is not always desirable. Know your value, worth and purpose...and know them without apology.

Rev. Larry Walker, Jr.

30. CHOOSE WISELY

The Prophet:

"In life, there's always a way in, just as there is a way out...It comes down to where you are standing & the direction you choose to go."

Untruan Grant

The Preacher:

There are many ways to reach a destination. Take time to evaluate where you stand... and then choose WISELY.

Rev. Larry Walker, Jr.

31. THE LONG WAY

The Prophet:

"There is no one "right" way as long as you learn along the way...the question is Should we always have to take the longest route to learn?"

Untruan Grant

The Preacher:

Learning, acquiring wisdom and the proper application of it make whatever route you choose, the right one for you. Often, we make the journey longer than it has to be.

Rev. Larry Walker, Jr.

32. LEAVE FOOTPRINTS

The Prophet:

"Leave a road less traveled leaving footprints to success, for others to appreciate the example left for them to follow."

Untruan Grant

The Preacher:

I like trails more than highways. The less travelled path leaves more to appreciate and more for me to leave to share in appreciation. Leave footprints, not breadcrumbs.

Rev. Larry Walker, Jr.

33. WATCHING

The Prophet:

"Someone is always watching and paying attention...Show the best version of yourself; leaving your true expression behind."

Untruan Grant

The Preacher:

Someone is always watching...sometimes the most important ones are our children. Take a good look at your future. It's in the reflection in the eyes of the child looking at you.

Rev. Larry Walker, Jr.

34. PAINT THE PICTURE

The Prophet:

"Paint the picture that you see of yourself & become it…After all, you are what you see of you. Add color in the midst of it all. Brighten it up a bit."

Untruan Grant

The Preacher:

Paint with broad strokes, but also with intimate detail. Brighten up the dark seasons in your life. A little color can add radiance to your life.

Rev. Larry Walker, Jr.

35. BEST VERSION

The Prophet:

"The best version of you is yet to be seen...You are a much bigger picture."

Untruan Grant

The Preacher:

Don't use a microscope to see who you are, when a telescope is what is required. Big pictures require bigger tools and equipment. Look beyond your horizons.

Rev. Larry Walker, Jr.

36. VISION & CLARITY

The Prophet:

"Your vision only becomes clear, once you reach a state of peace within yourself, to see things only as you can."

Untruan Grant

The Preacher:

Clarity is accomplished when peace is achieved. Perspective is everything. Peace is not the absence of conflict, it is steadfast commitment in the midst of conflict.

Rev. Larry Walker, Jr.

37. WHAT MAKES YOU, U

The Prophet:

"There is a reason nobody else sees things quite like you do...It's up to you to make your perspective clear."

Untruan Grant

The Preacher:

The reason you see things the way you do, is what makes you who you are. Wiping away dust, dirt and filth will definitely help you see clearer.

Rev. Larry Walker, Jr.

38. TIME IS NO FRIEND

The Prophet:

"Time seeks no friends, so you better learn to be friends with it. Maximize it if you can."

Untruan Grant

The Preacher:

Time is always too brief. It moves faster than you can imagine. It doesn't care to make friends. Make the best of it! Be FRIENDLY!

Rev. Larry Walker, Jr.

39. RESPECT TIME

The Prophet:

"Time is one thing that has no respect. You will learn it is best not to disrespect it..."

Untruan Grant

The Preacher:

Account for every moment you live and make every moment count. Evaluate your use of time. Now, tell me how you're living?

Rev. Larry Walker, Jr.

40. WILL POWER

The Prophet:

"To maximize your will power, you first must fully exercise your effort."

Untruan Grant

The Preacher:

Your impact will be measured by your power. Your power will be fueled by your actions. Get busy in the gym of life.

Rev. Larry Walker, Jr.

41. I AM GREAT

The Prophet:

"Say to yourself I am great & I love you daily then get out and be what you have told yourself today."

Untruan Grant

The Preacher:

Self-talk is Real Talk. I am and I love who I am, because of Him who made me to be, what I am becoming.

Rev. Larry Walker, Jr.

42. DO IT!

The Prophet:

"Whatever it is you see in yourself to do, Do It!...How else will you ever make your dreams come true."

Untruan Grant

The Preacher:

Insight becomes reality, when you exercise faith to put what is necessary in motion. Get moving. It is Already Done!

Rev. Larry Walker, Jr.

43. LAYERS

The Prophet:

"Growth comes with shedding layers to see our better self...the better we can see, the better we will see ourselves doing."

Untruan Grant

The Preacher:

Peel back the layers...remove the piles. Vision is best after some personal gardening or construction work.

Rev. Larry Walker, Jr.

44. CAPTURE MOMENTS

The Prophet:

"Capture every loving moment you possibly can...There comes a time when you have to look back to recall all the love you really have in life."

Untruan Grant

The Preacher:

Cameras capture a moment in time, but your heart stores millions of memories that only you can truly see and appreciate.

Rev. Larry Walker, Jr.

45. MEMORY BANKS

The Prophet:

"Collect & do the things that warm your heart, creating a happy memory bank, full of deposits."

Untruan Grant

The Preacher:

My bank account is not nearly as full as my memory bank. The things I treasure are invaluable.

Rev. Larry Walker, Jr.

46. POTENTIAL

The Prophet:

"Once you become open to your potential, the Universe open up to you to making everything possible. The greatness inside you waits on you to live outside of you."

Untruan Grant

The Preacher:

There is a future world that is only made possible because of you and your greatness waiting to be released.

Rev. Larry Walker, Jr.

47. DIMMER SWITCH

The Prophet:

"Your success is not meant only for you. It is for so many others to model...So don't pull the dimmer switch on your own light."

Untruan Grant

The Preacher:

A dimmer switch should only be meant for someone else. You were meant to shine, so others will see the light and reflect it.

Rev. Larry Walker, Jr.

48. SHINE ON

The Prophet:

"Allow your light to shine on high like the sun. Give a good view of what possible looks like...Keep rising!"

Untruan Grant

The Preacher:

Possibilities are exposed when light is applied. Remove all the darkness and with warmth, like heat, will continue to rise.

Rev. Larry Walker, Jr.

49. YOUR LENS

The Prophet:

"Through the lenses of your own frames, your reality awaits you. Look Forward."

Untruan Grant

The Preacher:

The frame holds the lens...but you hold the frame. See clearly. Put on the glasses of your life and enjoy.

Rev. Larry Walker, Jr.

50. BREAKTHROUGH

The Prophet:

"Push through until you break through... You've been rooted to rise above it all."

Untruan Grant

The Preacher:

Persevere and overcome...You have been planted to bloom. The roots beneath the ground allow for the flowers above.

Rev. Larry Walker, Jr.

51. MAXIMUM POWER

The Prophet:

"Maximum power is never achieved with minimum effort. Engage your maximum to better your best."

Untruan Grant

The Preacher:

Your impact will be measured by your power. Your power will be fueled by your actions. Get busy in the gym of life!

Rev. Larry Walker, Jr.

52. PREPARATION

The Prophet:

*"In life, prepare yourself & position yourself;
knowing that your defining moment awaits you."*

Untruan Grant

The Preacher:

At the intersection of preparation and positioning, you will find a street sign that says, "You have arrived".

Rev. Larry Walker, Jr.

53. SHARE

The Prophet:

"Always be willing to share the information you have inside; maybe it will serve to ignite someone else."

Untruan Grant

The Preacher:

Sharing, truly is caring. If you care about being a real catalyst for positive change, stoke the fire for good.

Rev. Larry Walker, Jr.

54. DREAMING

The Prophet:

"Your dream will not just come to you... You must work at it & go get it."

Untruan Grant

The Preacher:

Hard work allows for great achievement. Pursue with passion and a vengeance, the dream that is yours alone.

Rev. Larry Walker, Jr

55. WALK IT OUT

The Prophet:

"Be willing to walk out your dreams, rather than laying down to sleep on them...They are real & you have the will to bring them into existence."

Untruan Grant

The Preacher:

Rest is preparation for action and sleep is a reward for activity. Walk with a swagger that says my dreams are something special. Here I come!

Rev. Larry Walker, Jr.

56. OBSTACLES

The Prophet:

"Only you can tell yourself what you can & cannot do... Only you can strengthen yourself in what you will do and apply it to your success in life."

Untruan Grant

The Preacher:

You are the only obstacle preventing you from achieving what you desire. Strengthen yourself for the task ahead. Your life is not for the weak.

Rev. Larry Walker, Jr.

57. RENEWAL

The Prophet:

"The renewal of your mind changes everything about you and allows you to see the better in you; but you have to build on it continuously."

Untruan Grant

The Preacher:

Renewal, refreshing, reviving and redirection all start with a mindset that says I can do better. It's a foundational truth on which to build.

Rev. Larry Walker, Jr.

58. REWARDS

The Prophet:

"As you do your very best, you'll find men can give an Award, but it's God who gives the Reward...Keep at it!"

Untruan Grant

The Preacher:

I have received many awards, but the greatest reward is yet to come. Servanthood comes with a "well done" when we reach the end of our journey.

Rev. Larry Walker, Jr.

59. WORK

The Prophet:

"Keep working at your goals. What you can't see, never goes unnoticed in the sight of God."

Untruan Grant

The Preacher:

Isn't it funny that you never get paid for a day you didn't work or earn as time off? Live each day as if you worked for God. He pays EVERY day.

Rev. Larry Walker, Jr.

60. LAUGHTER

The Prophet:

"The best medicine is laughter…Take it daily. You'll feel better by the end of each day."

Untruan Grant

The Preacher:

Medicine helps cure what ails you. The best medicine is free. Laughter makes everyone feel better.

Rev. Larry Walker, Jr.

61. TO BE GREAT

The Prophet:

"To go somewhere great in life, you must be willing to be used anywhere in life."

Untruan Grant

The Preacher:

Usefulness is about availability and willingness. Don't put restrictions on how and where God will use you. He knows the road ahead.

Rev. Larry Walker, Jr.

62. BE A LIGHT

The Prophet:

"Be a shining light, no matter where you must stand...someone is always lost and you could be that guiding hand."

Untruan Grant

The Preacher:

A lighthouse is never found underground. Someone is always seeking direction...if they could only see the light.

Rev. Larry Walker, Jr.

63. ACCEPT STRUGGLE

The Prophet:

"Accepting your struggles with the same energy as your blessings makes you better prepared to accept the rewards in life."

Untruan Grant

The Preacher:

Struggle builds strength. You don't get strong to do hard work; you do hard work to get strong. Mow your yard, so your life will be beautiful.

Rev. Larry Walker, Jr.

64. BLESSING BURDEN

The Prophet:

"The blessing is never too much to receive, so don't allow the weight to feel like more than you can bear."

Untruan Grant

The Preacher:

The burden of blessings is that sometimes we feel like we don't deserve them. Being a conduit of blessings can feel like a burden we cannot bear. They are meant to flow through, not just to.

Rev. Larry Walker, Jr.

65. DREAM REALITY

The Prophet:

"Follow your dreams until they become your reality in life or they will become a living nightmare."

Untruan Grant

The Preacher:

Dreams left unrealized become nightmares of "what if?". Chase your dreams...they are not trying to outrun you.

Rev. Larry Walker, Jr.

66. DO YOU WANT IT?

The Prophet:

"Nothing is given. You're going to have to work at everything. Determine in advance if you really want it or not."

Untruan Grant

The Preacher:

Determine in advance if the effort is worthwhile. Nothing is more frustrating than wasted time, effort and energy. Do you really want what you say?

Rev. Larry Walker, Jr.

67. THE BEST THINGS

The Prophet:

"The best things just don't come. You are going to have to work for them. Your effort changes things."

Untruan Grant

The Preacher:

Nothing happens without effort. Sweat and tears are the results of hard work. Hard work is the impetus for radicle change.

Rev. Larry Walker, Jr.

68. START ANEW

The Prophet:

"If an end is already damaged, cut it off so new growth can begin."

Untruan Grant

The Preacher:

If something is dead, bury it, destroy it or get rid of it. New growth can only begin when you reach the end of the old and decide to begin anew.

Rev. Larry Walker, Jr.

69. A BLESSED NEW DAY

The Prophet:

"You are blessed with a new day daily. Be as new as the previous day, before you decide to take on a yesterday that will not return."

Untruan Grant

The Preacher:

Newness, a fresh start or a new beginning are a blessed gifts that says open me. Yesterday can never return. It is a forever gone memory of what once was.

Rev. Larry Walker, Jr.

70. YOUTHFULNESS

The Prophet:

"Carrying old things into a new day , will have you acting old. Be young as your new day, because you really are."

Untruan Grant

The Preacher:

Youth is fleeting. Don't act older than you are, because one day you will be. Approach each day with new vigor; because as we age, the things we carry become heavier.

Rev. Larry Walker, Jr.

71. RESPECT TIME

The Prophet:

"No matter the storm nor when they come, you have the power to brighten the day, just as the sun."

Untruan Grant

The Preacher:

It doesn't matter what you are going through. What makes the difference is what you allow to get to you. Discover a ray of sunshine in each new day.

Rev. Larry Walker, Jr.

72. RE-CREATE

The Prophet:

"The things you strongly dislike, you may find yourself recreating in your own life. Don't allow your past to make up your today."

Untruan Grant

The Preacher:

Be careful what you duplicate. Accidents are the invention of real monsters. Past mistakes re-duplicated are no longer just mistakes.

Rev. Larry Walker, Jr.

73. BE POSITIVE

The Prophet:

"Keep your own POSITIVE state of being. It controls the state around you."

Untruan Grant

The Preacher:

Control you own thinking. Critical thinking is no longer being taught and common sense is no longer common...and it is no longer counted in cents.

Rev. Larry Walker, Jr.

74. NEW THINGS

The Prophet:

"Creating a new experience in a old environment will cultivate young minds for a new environment to build."

Untruan Grant

The Preacher:

Building on a foundation formerly built, reaps rewards not formerly achieved. Same place, New energy – different results. New things can be created from old ideas.

Rev. Larry Walker, Jr.

75. SELFCARE

The Prophet:

"Many people have attempted everything under the sun; overlooking the obvious of giving themselves a shot at helping themselves. You're stronger than what you give yourself credit for."

Untruan Grant

The Preacher:

Self-care and improvement should be the goal of every human being. Then we can take better care of someone else. We are most strong when we can carry our own load.

Rev. Larry Walker, Jr.

76. STAND FIRM

The Prophet:

"Stand firm like a tree, and do not allow the conditions surrounding you to break you. You will produce oxygen in a toxic environment."

Untruan Grant

The Preacher:

Stand strong in the midst of tumultuous winds. Stay rooted and planted and when the storm is all over, you will still be providing the necessary ingredients for growth.

Rev. Larry Walker, Jr.

77. UNLOCKING DOORS

The Prophet:

"Your effort holds the key to the story of your life. Push forward as you see it through."

Untruan Grant

The Preacher:

Keys unlock many doors, but only your key unlocks your door. Also remember, not every closed door is locked.

Rev. Larry Walker, Jr.

78. LESSONS

The Prophet:

*"Your lessons may not be as attractive as your blessings...but what looks good **to** you isn't always good **for** you."*

Untruan Grant

The Preacher:

Lessons are blessings in disguise. The more you learn; the more blessed you are. Learn the difference between what is good for you and what is good to you.

Rev. Larry Walker, Jr.

79. THE END

The Prophet:

"The end of the story is not visible at the beginning of the book. Dare to go through all the chapters to know the full story."

Untruan Grant

The Preacher:

Only God sees the end from the beginning. Just keep turning the pages. We are just the readers; not the author. It's a good book. I read the ending.

Rev. Larry Walker, Jr.

ABOUT THE AUTHOR

Rev. Larry Walker, Jr. was born in Indianapolis, Indiana to Larry Walker, Sr and Christina Henard. He grew up with four brothers and one sister in a loving home during a time of racial tensions and forced integration.

He has lived in Louisville, KY, Nashville, TN, Atlanta, GA and Stamford, CT. He moved to the Dallas/Ft. Worth Metroplex in 1982; the place he now calls home. He has been Executive Director at Inner-City Solutions, Inc, and a leader at several Non-profit organizations, including Anthem Strong Families and Matthew 25:40 Project.

He is the Founder of Living God's Way Ministries, Inc. and The Gideon Group of North Texas and has a heart for our neighbors without homes, the formerly incarcerated and veterans.

Rev. Walker describes himself as a *connector* and prides himself on being an all-inclusive community collaborator and leader. He is fond of saying:

"I know a whole lot of people most people would like to know; the kind of people everybody should want to know. They are the kind of people who know it is more important to be KIND, than to be known."

His calling is to bring them together.

ABOUT THE AUTHOR

Untruan Grant is a father, mentor, life coach, entrepreneur, author and motivational public speaker who teaches people the importance of perseverance and speaking "his truth" of how he overcame the tragedies he was born into, including abandonment, physical, verbal and mental abuse.

Untruan has made it his life's mission to educate and mentor those who come from a background of brokenness. Untruan is a member of Urban Specialists' OGU movement which teaches individuals like himself, who are from urban communities, on how to use their influence to stop senseless violence and how to change the current toxic culture of the world.

In addition to mentoring, Untruan is a public speaker who speaks on topics relating to youth empowerment, black mental health, overcoming odds, community development and more. Untruan has been invited to speak at Urban Specialists' OGU Movement and many other community events.

Untruan is also a member of Tyro Champion Dads - Anthem Strong Families; an organization that empowers fathers to be their absolute best for their children and families.

THE PREACHER AND THE STREET PROPHET

Rev. Larry Walker, Jr.

Untruan Grant

THE PREACHER & THE STREET PROPHET

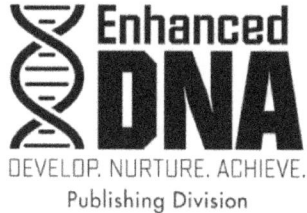

Denola M. Burton
DenolaBurton@EnhancedDNA1.com
www.EnhancedDNAPublishing.com

www.ingramcontent.com/pod-product-compliance
Lightning Source LLC
LaVergne TN
LVHW021407080426
835508LV00020B/2486